आईना ज़मीर का देखा

(50 ग़ज़लें)

ON LOOKING INTO THE MIRROR OF CONSCIENCE

आईना ज़मीर का देखा
(50 ग़ज़लें)

ON LOOKING INTO THE MIRROR OF CONSCIENCE

Kumar Shiv

in Translation

Publications

KALPAZ PUBLICATIONS

DELHI-110052

ON LOOKING INTO THE MIRROR OF CONSCIENCE

ISBN : 81-7835-589-2

Published in 2007 in India by
Kalpaz Publications
C-30, Satyawati Nagar, Delhi-110052
E-mail : Kalpaz@hotmail.com

Laser Typesetting at : Master Computers, Delhi
Printed at : Salasar Imaging System, Delhi

To,

My wife pramila,

The presiding deity of my life

Acknowledgements

I am extremely grateful to His Excellency Rashtrapati Ji Dr. APJ Abdul Kalam for his kind blessings.

I am beholden to Hon'ble Justice Shivaraj V. Patil who was kind enough to agree to write the foreword inspite of his busy schedule.

I am thankful to Hon'ble Justice Bhagwati Prasad, Hon'ble Justice R.S. Chauhan, Dr. Mukesh Sharma, Sh. Guman Singh, Sh.S.S. Kothari, Smt. Anita Kothari, Sh. U.C. Barupal and Sh. Arvind Sharma who have helped in many ways to make this book grow.

Thanks are also due to Sh. Garg of Gyan Books Pvt. Ltd. who worked hard to bring the book out attractively and in time.

KUMAR SHIV

A-10, GANDHI NAGAR
JAIPUR (RAJASTHAN)

June 29, 2006.

A.P.J. Abdul Kalam

Rashtrapati Bhavan
New Delhi - 110004
June 2, 2006

Dear Shri Justice Sharma,

I have seen your collection of poems which reflect the images, one sees "On Looking into the Mirror of Conscience". I have found the poems to be examples of sensitivity and reflection. The following lines are inspiring :-

"His sights are set on the sky,
And on his lips are prayers;
The efforts are untiring,
And there's courage enough to dare."

My best wishes for your thoughts and poetic composition.

With best wishes.

Yours sincerely,

Shri Justice Shiv Kumar Sharma
Judge
Rajasthan High Court
A-10, Gandhi Nagar
JAIPUR.

From the Desk of Translator

He embarked upon a journey par excellence, an Odyssey of a passionate dream, at a time that was Six decades apart. Growing with the country rising to 'The New Dawn' and a Nation that had to learn it all over again, being extra-ordinarily perceptive was nascent to him. A true child of the Nation, Shiv Kumar Sharma has shared the sweet and sour tastes, myriad shades of colors as well as azar shadows, poignant ambitions and inherent rebellious anger, with the India after freedom. The poetic tradition of calling a spade a spade did not die with the Raj, but it grew with the changing dimensions of truth. How could Shiv remain untouched by the truth! With the wounded psyche of a fragile and vulnerable Mother's sincere son, his start on the wings of contemporary poetry that regretted the Mother's plights and rebelled against the plunderers of Her pride, was as spontaneous as youth. It was not long before Shiv Metamorphosed into 'Kumar Shiv'.

Born at Kota, Rajasthan, the city blessed with mighty river Chambal, Kumar Shiv is true embodiment of the torrent but nurturing energy of flowing water. His verses torment the mind with candid truth-telling and soothe the soul with melodious attribute of a song, peculiarly rendering it in single stroke. Kumar Shiv has been fortunate to go down the history of Indian stage poetry having had the opportunity to share the dais with renowned names such as Dushyant Kumar, Sarveshwar Dayal Saxena, Ramanath Awasthi, Gopal Das Neeraj, Dr.

Basheer Badra, Nida Fazli and likes. Despite the humbling presence of these stalwarts, Kumar Shiv could carve a niche of his own. Containing the contrast with rather solemn profession of a leading legal practitioner, Kumar Shiv not only made innumerable appearances on All India Radio and Doordarshan, but also featured regularly in the esteemed weekly Dharmyug. With three poetic compilations published as "Shankh Ret Ke Chehre", "Pankh Dhoop Ke" and "Hilte Haath Darakhton Ke", Kumar Shiv deserves accolades for his relentless commitment to poetry. Nostalgically recalling the heydays of Kumar Shiv's poetry, the acclaimed Urdu poet and critic from Jodhpur, Rajasthan, Sheen Kaaf Nizam proclaims his exclusivity as a poet loved by both the readers as well as the listeners of poems.

Shiv Kumar Sharma's elevation to the hallowed portals of the Rajasthan High Court earned him the enviable status and a new name - Justice Shiv Kumar Sharma, in the year 1996. Though he proved to be a true son of the soil here as well, however the illustrious career of a Judge also marginalized his poetry. Justice Shiv Kumar Sharma has certainly earned kudos as an extraordinary just judge but the humble and levelheaded conscience that he possessed, has maintained the throne of justice in place; beneath himself and not on the head. Consequently, the flame and fervor he was born with could not be doused, so what it partially invisible under the files and muffled amidst the voices of law, order and judgments.

The collection of **50 of his latest** poems I have the honor here to introduce, is nothing but a mere testimony of Kumar Shiv's eternal affair with poetry. The incessant creative energy that he has always been impregnated with, has emerged again to woo the ink after a long gap of almost **three** decades.

It is said that the poetry is not what mind does but what dawns upon the mind, instead. Kumar Shiv's poems are virtual transliteration of the morally and socially upright sensibilities which enlighten his perception, exactly in the similar fashion as the twilight of down unfurls new wonders in a garden. The "..........." Largely expresses the poet's angst against the dismal shifts of value paradigms in contemporary system and society. There is a sweeping presence of scathing satire and brooding lamentations of the morality and prudence that has fallen from the grace. A few poems out rightly proclaim the poet's contempt against the feudalistic shadows that still shroud the country's system.

"Who says I am ignorant
Of the Sovereign power;
I stand up and my head bows
In awe and reverence."

(... trans. poem no. 1)

"The darkness came on roll,
With the Sire's arrival in town;
The serpents stirred their hoods,
Snake charmers paced up and down."

(...trans. poem no. 49)

There are others that agonize upon the deplorable state of affairs in public life:-

"The trees are sad,
In silence the leaves lie;
The dew-drenched garden
Wore the butterflies."

(...trans. poem no. 12)

The compilation holds a judicious balance with several poems earnestly striving to urge the reader to struggle against the depressive truths. The following translated stanza from poem no.14 also reminds the 'mighty pen':-

"He will rise up,
With tight fists and stout stand;
Someone will again stand up,
Holding the mighty pen."

(...trans. poem no. 14)

The range of reactions to system and society and dimensions of human emotions that the compilation incorporates, actually makes it worthy of being christened as an Omnibus of the poet. Here he touches the pulse of women issues, and there he goes romantic with serenading sonnets. It is irresistible for me to invoke some examples here:-

"On the henna painted hands,
That's what the destiny wrote;
Grindstone, fodder, broom, sand
Pots, fuel and smoke."

(...trans. poem no. 11)

"The night listens to the flute,
And the swanging of the bamboo forest;
It yawns and stretches,
With both the hands in air."

(...trans. poem no. 5)

Kumar Shiv, standing up to his name, has thereby weaved a wonderful flag, which not only marks the acerbic 'truths' but also adorns the 'beauty' of emotions. The simplicity of the craft and lucidity of language ensures that this set of poems touches the soul, amuses the heart and tills the fertile soil of conscience too.

Kumar Shiv originally writes in common man's Hindustani which reveals his deft linguistic grip on Hindi as well as authentic Urdu. It is his generosity that for the benefit of non-Devnagri readers, he decided to translate the poems in English. In a chance encounter with my humble self, he discussed the idea of coming up with a bilingual or diglot edition; but lamented the dearth of time. Needless to say, the divine duty to render justice keeps him inextricably busy. It was as if foreordained, there is no other way to explain the courage I mustered to attempt a feat bigger than my shoes. As the luck would have it, out of nowhere but spontaneity, he offered me to translate the poems. It was an opportunity I could not help grabbing gleefully. I do not even want to try my impoverished lexicon to thank Justice Shiv Kumar Sharma for his magnanimous gesture. All I could do was to give my best to hold the faith entrusted by a poet. I have endeavored to harmonize with the soul while translating the poems, albeit owing to my limited knowledge of English, it has been an ordeal for me. I therefore extend an advance apology for slips and inaccuracies which I am sure to have committed aplenty.

Dr. Mukesh Sharma

Dr. Justice Shivaraj V. Patil
Member
(Former Judge, Supreme Court of India)

National Human Rights Commission
Faridkot House, Copernicus Marg
New Delhi-110 001
Phone : 91-11-2338 7328
Fax: 91-11-2338 4863
E-mail: patilsv@nic.in

पुरोवाक्

मेरे सुहृद श्री शिव कुमार शर्मा की यह सरस काव्य कृति 'आईना ज़मीर का देखा' उनकी चुनिंदा पचास ग़ज़लों का संकलन है। ये ग़ज़लें विभिन्न विषयों पर हैं पर उनके केन्द्र में आदमी है। कवि की पैनी निगाहों से ज़िन्दगी के हर पहलू का जायज़ा लिया गया है। संघर्षरत, बेबस आदमी की तकलीफ, उसकी खुद्दारी, अनुभव में आती विसंगतियाँ, प्रकृति के बदलते रंग, और जिजीविषा के कई रंगों से सजीव चित्र उकेरती इन ग़ज़लों को पढ़ते हुए आस-पास की दुनिया, उसकी जद्दोजहद, हार जीत और टूटते आदमी की उलझनों और इन सबके बीच आशा की कोपलें पाठक के मन में कौंध जाती हैं।

जब मैं राजस्थान उच्च न्यायालय का मुख्य न्यायाधीश था, तब मुझे न्यायमूर्ति श्री शिवकुमार शर्मा जी को निकटता से जानने का अवसर मिला। जीवन के प्रति उनके समृद्ध अनुभव और एक कवि हृदय की महान कल्पना उनके व्यवहार एवं निर्णयों में प्रतिबिम्बित होती है। यही मानवीय संवेदना के साथ पूर्ण न्याय है। मैंने उनमें कानून और कविता का अनोखा संगम पाया है। श्री शर्मा मस्तिष्क से न्यायाधीश तथा हृदय से कवि हैं जो एक दुर्लभ संयोग है।

शिव जी के शब्दों में कहें तो

देखने में जो तुमको बुझ गए से लगते हैं,
अब भी उन चरागों में रोशनी बकाया है।

शिव जी की नज़र से कुछ भी नहीं छुपता। मूल्यों के गिरावट के जमाने में

अगर कोई बेवफा हुआ है, क्यों उसको तोहमत हुजूर दें हम,
ग़लतबयानी दग़ा, बुराई, ये आजकल की जरूरतें हैं।

प्यार और प्रकृति से सराबोर ये पंक्तियाँ मोहक धुन छेड़ती हैं और गुनगुनाने को प्रेरित करती हैं :-

बजता है बांसों का जंगल सुनती है शहनाई रात,
अपने दोनों हाथ उठाकर लेती है अंगड़ाई रात।

....

पलकें हैं बोझिल-बोझिल और चेहरे पर सिन्दूर लगा,
सुबह पूछती है सूरज से बोलो कहाँ बिताई रात।

या फिर इन पंक्तियों पर गौर करें :-

गालों पर गीली रेखाएँ रोकर सोया होगा चाँद,
ये तारे हैं चाँद के आँसू कितना रोया होगा चाँद।

....

रात अकेली तट पर बैठी खोले केश हवाओं के,
अपना तुमने और रात ने अपना धोया होगा चाँद।

शिव जी की ग़ज़लो को पढ़ते हुए मैंने मानसिक धरातल पर लम्बी यात्रा तय की जो देश और काल दोनों आयामों में फैली थी। इस यात्रा के कुछ पड़ावों का उल्लेख करने से मैं अपने को रोक नहीं सकूंगा। गाँव का चित्र खींचती एक ग़ज़ल थोड़े से शब्दों में बहुत कुछ कह डालती है :

कर्ज़ दादा का पिता पर फिर पिता का पुत्र पर,
वादों, प्रतिवादों, मुकदमों कुर्कियों का गाँव था।

....

खेत में गेहूँ हरे थे, झाड़ियों में बेर थे,
ककड़ियों का और खट्टी इमलियों का गाँव था।
कातती चरखे, सुनाती थी जो मीठी लोरियाँ,
सूत जैसे बाल वाली नानियों का गाँव था।

ज़िन्दगी में हमें तरह-तरह के लोग मिलते हैं। उनसे समर्थन, चुनौती, प्यार सब कुछ मिलता है और कदम आगे बढ़ते रहते हैं। आदमी के निर्माण में इन सबका योगदान रहता है।

साथ थे शिकवे गिले आलोचनाएँ साथ थीं।
थे कई आशीष भी, शुभकामनाएं साथ थीं।
इस तरह तय हो सका काँटो भरा यह पथ यहाँ,
हाथ सर पर था बुजुर्गो का, दुआएँ साथ थीं।

बदलता समय, आज की परेशानियाँ और विसंगतियो का प्रभावशाली चित्रण करते शिवजी के ये शब्द पाठक के मन पर गहरी छाप छोड़ते हैं :

जब भी वक्त बदलता है कुछ ऐसा ही हो जाता है,
नावें तो मिल जाती हैं पर होते उन पर पाल नहीं।

....

चाहें जितना भी हँस लें मुस्कालें जीभर कर गा लें,
यह है ऐसा वक़्त आजकल कोई भी खुशहाल नहीं।

परंपरा और परिवर्तन का द्वन्द्व शिवजी की गई ग़ज़लों में मिलता है। मिसाल के तौर पर चिरपरिचित घर, घर के लोग, घरनी जो अब विसरते जा रहे हैं, उनको याद दिलाते शिव जी कहते हैं :

गीली लकड़ी चूल्हा-चौका चिमटा बेलन और धुआँ
भीगा अंजन, बजते कंगन यह गोरा तन और धुआँ।

अभी भी आशा बनी हुई है कि

मुट्ठियों को बांधकर तन कर खड़ा हो जाएगा,
फिर यहाँ कोई कलम लेकर खड़ा हो जाएगा।

प्रकृति को परखती नज़र ही यह चित्र उकेर सकती हैः

सूरज को जब ग्रहण लगेगा दिन बैसाखी पर सरकेगा,
तुलसी की पूजा कर लेगी रख लेगी उपवास दुपहरी।
बादल के पीछे मत जाओ, सूरज तुम्हें शपथ है इसकी,
तुम बिछुड़ोगे तो वियोग में ले लेगी सन्यास दुपहरी।

नगरीय जीवन में उद्योग, अफरा-तफरी, विषमता मिल कर हमें क्या दे रहे है? इस प्रश्न का एक सटीक और मजबूर कर देने वाला चित्र भूला नहीं जा सकता :

किस तरह का शहर है यहाँ हर तरफ है धुआँ ही धुआँ,
जंगलो की सी आबोहवा भेड़ियों के नियम कायदे।

या, निम्न पंक्तियों को देखें :

सूरज को हुआ है क्या कृशकाय उजाला है,
डरता है अँधेरे से, असहाय उजाला है।

कवि मन के मन में आलोड़न है :

ख़ून को क्या हो गया है क्यों नहीं आता उबाल,
बन्द गलियों की नसों की, धमनियों को देख लें।

आज जीवन के सामने उभरते प्रश्नों को शब्द देते हुए कवि शिव कुमार जी, सब कुछ के बावजूद मानते हैं :

कभी तो बदलेगा बिगड़ा मौसम, ढलेगी ये लम्बी रात काली,
है हमको उम्मीद देख लेंगे, नए सवेरों की चहलकदमी।

मुझे न्यायमूर्ति शिवकुमार शर्मा जी के व्यक्तित्व एवं कृतित्व पर नाज़ और खुशी है। श्री शर्मा की ग़ज़लों को पढ़कर महामहिम राष्ट्रपति जी ने अपने उद्‌गार व्यक्त करते हुए लिखा है :-

"मैंने इन कविताओं में संवेदनशीलता और माननीय चिंतन की झलक पायी है।"

इनकी निम्न पक्तियाँ प्रेरणादायी हैं :-

His sights are set on the sky,
And on his lips are prayers;
The efforts are untiring,
And there's courage enough to dare.

मनुष्य, मनुष्य इसीलिए है कि वह संभावनाओ को देख पाता है और साकार कर पाता हैं। मनुष्य का यह विश्वास ही उसकी विकास यात्रा का आधार है। हमें भरोसा है कि आने वाला कल मंगलमय होगा। इसके लिए विवेक और सचेत कर्म की अपेक्षा होगी। 'आईना ज़मीर का देखा' हमें इसी बात की पहचान कराता है। आत्म-परीक्षण और आत्म विश्वास के लिए इस आवाह्न के लिए हम सब शिव जी के आभारी हैं। मेरी कामना है कि काव्य जगत में इस रचना का स्वागत हो। आम आदमी भी इन ग़ज़लों का भरपूर स्वाद ले सकेगा, इनकी सरल और धारदार भाषा बरबस मन को अंदर तक भिगो जाती है। श्री शर्मा जी ने अंग्रेजी और हिंदी दोनों भाषाओं में ग़ज़लों की रचना कर एक अनोखा प्रयोग किया है। दोनों भाषाओं में ग़ज़लों के होने से इनका आनंद हिंदी के साथ-साथ अंग्रेजी भाषियों को भी मिल सकेगा। मैं इस रचना के लिए शिव कुमार जी को हार्दिक बधाई देता हूँ। उन्होंने मुझे अपनी कविता के रसास्वादन का अवसर दिया इसके लिए मैं आभारी हूँ। मुझे पूरा विश्वास है कि उनकी लेखनी से आगे भी सशक्त रचनाएँ मिलेंगी। उनका मार्ग प्रशस्त हो तथा वे सुखी हों।

शुभास्ते सन्तु पन्थानः

सर्वे भवन्तु सुखिनः

आपके काव्यमयी अनुभूतियों एवं विचारों के लिए मेरी शुभकामनाएँ।

(शिवराज वी. पाटील)

(1)

Resplendent is the Lord's facade
Gloomy is his shadow
But the intoxicated coterie
And the poor plebeians are struck dumb.

Who says I am ignorant
Of the sovereign power
I have stood up and bowed
In awe and reverence.

To your simple eyes
They appear as if doused
Light in those lamps though
Still remains to glow.

The scribes are busy
Enlisting the lot
Who has brought gifts
Worth a thought.

It is fun and fiesta
In bejewelled stadia today;
Who is it who knows
What the unborn tomorrow holds.

Wherever crawls
The slippery trails of power
It breeds hungry serpents
And enchanting phantoms of desire.

(1)

सुर्ख़ साहबे–आलम, ज़र्द उनका साया है,
सिरफ़िरे हैं दरबारी, बेज़ुबां रियाया है।

सल्तनत के रुतबे से बेखबर नहीं हैं हम,
बाअदब खड़े होकर हमने सर झुकाया है।

देखने में जो तुमको बुझ गए से लगते हैं,
अब भी उन चराग़ों में रोशनी बक़ाया है।

लिख रहे हैं कारिन्दे, बन रही हैं फ़हरिस्तें,
बेशक़ीमती तोहफे साथ कौन लाया है।

जश्न और जलसे हैं आज शामियानों में,
कल न जाने क्या होगा कौन जान पाया है।

जिस तरफ़ भी जाता है रास्ता सियासत का,
अजदहे हैं, फिसलन है, धूप और छाया है।

(2)

Buried in my eyes are
A few dilapidated buildings of yore;
You could not ever decipher
The epitaphs that my tears wrote.

Wrapped up have I always been
In the fragrant muse;
It's all because of your benevolence
That my smiles eclipse my woes.

Entrapped amidst charlatans
My life has turned into a mime;
Hearts abound with hatred yet
Love is sold a dime a dozen.

Overwhelmed in fear
Are the birds hidden in the nests;
None are happy here in the jungle
Adversities exhaust every quest.

Why should I incriminate him,
Who has turned traitor;
Abuses, evils and betrayals
Have become today's necessities.

(2)

हमारी आँखों में गुज़रे कल की गिरी हुई कुछ इमारतें हैं,
नहीं जो तुम पढ़ सके कभी भी, वो आँसुओं की इबारतें हैं।

तसव्वुरी के महकते लमहे रहे हमेशा करीब अपने,
दुखों में भी मुस्करा रहे हैं, ये सब तुम्हारी इनायतें हैं।

तमाशबीनों के बीच रहकर यह ज़िन्दगी बन गई तमाशा,
दिलों में नफ़रत, मगर नुमायाँ हुई यहाँ पर मोहब्बतें है।

हैं ख़ौफ़ से बाख़बर, दरख़्तों के घोंसलों में छिपे परिन्दे,
कोई भी जंगल में खुश नहीं है, जिधर भी देखो मुसीबतें हैं।

अगर कोई बेवफ़ा हुआ है, क्यों उसको तोहमत हुजूर दें हम,
ग़लतबयानी दग़ा, बुराई, ये आजकल की ज़रूरतें हैं।

(3)

There were the brave knights who warred,
Beheaded by enemy but combated undeterred.

There were also the sycophants of power,
Who reared on their shoulders selfish sunflowers.

The ones injured by the broken branch that fell free,
Were those who preferred the shadows of the tree.

Were all in the house like programmed toys?
I wonder how their hands clapped together for the same ploy!

Strange was that era when they stood tall,
Who walked around with no backbones at all!

(3)

थे जो जाँबाज बहादुर वो जंग करते थे,
सर तो कट जाते थे लेकिन कबन्ध लड़ते थे।

मगर थे ऐसे भी धड़ शाह की हुकूमत में,
कि जिनके काँधों पे सूरजमुखी महकते थे।

जो टूटी शाख से दबकर लहुलुहान हुए,
वो लोग पेड़ की छाया तले ठहरते थे।

सभा में क्या सभी चाबी भरे खिलौने थे,
सभी के हाथ वहाँ एक साथ बजते थे।

अजीब दौर था, उनके हुए थे कद ऊँचे,
जो लोग रीढ़ की हड्डी हटाए फिरते थे।

(4)

I was paper – the rusted pins were company,
The select few stood by – and they were not many.

The mid-day Sun was scorching and it was a long way to go,
I did find shelter but the heated tin would not forgo.

Now descended light, now darkness swathed my courtyard,
Now pleasure, now miseries-such days trapped my heart.

Multiple masks hid the face of friend,
Elusive remained the bonhomie–no matter how long he did stand.

Now I often remember the comfort of my father's arms,
How good were those days when I had my mother and sisters around!

(4)

कागज़ थे हम, जंग लगे कुछ आलपिनों का साथ रहा,
साथ रहा, कुछ ख़ास ख़ास और इने गिनों का साथ रहा।

दोपहरी थी, तेज धूप थी और रास्ता लम्बा था,
छाँव मिली थी लेकिन तपते हुए टिनों का साथ रहा।

कभी रोशनी उतरी, कभी अँधेरे से डूबा आँगन,
कभी सुखों और कभी दुखों से घिरे दिनों का साथ रहा।

दोस्त मिले ऐसे जिनके चेहरों पर कई मुखौटे थे,
अपनापन मिल सका नहीं चाहे महिनों का साथ रहा।

दादा और पिता की छाया याद बहुत आती है अब,
कितने अच्छे थे वो दिन जब माँ–बहिनों का साथ रहा।

(5)

Adorned with broken stars,
Trapped in the threads of maladies
I spent this lonely night so bizarre,
Singing swan-songs and threnodies.

The night listens to the flute,
And the swaying of the bamboo forest;
It yawns and stretches,
With both hands in the air.

I know not why,
My heart mopes;
It feels as if
The night is a mere reflection of the yore!

Eyelids learnt to carry,
The weight of the moon;
In the pots of eyes did I rear,
The memories' fragrant bloom.

The face besmeared with vermilion,
And the leaden eyes;
The Morning asked the Sun,
Where it had spent the night.

(5)

टूटे तारे और दुखों के धागों ने उलझाई रात,
हमने ग़ज़लें गाकर तनहाई में यहाँ बिताई रात,

बजता है बाँसों का जंगल सुनती है शहनाई रात,
अपने दोनों हाथ उठाकर लेती है अंगड़ाई रात।

जाने क्यों बेवजह कभी भी मन उदास हो जाता है,
ऐसा लगता है जैसे हो माजी की परछाई रात।

माहताब का बोझ उठाना सीखीं खुली हुईं पलकें,
हमने आँखों के गमलों में यादों से महकाई रात।

पलकें हैं वोझिल वोझिल और चेहरे पर सिन्दूर लगा,
सुबह पूछती है सूरज से बोलो कहाँ बिताई रात।

(6)

Sunken eyes and rickety ribs,
Sick and tired that village was;
Decaying fingers and moribund souls,
Oh! How decadent that village was!

The farms of the village,
All mortgaged in red ledgers;
The homes entangled in webs
All occupied by spiders that village was.

Grandpa's debt on father,
Father's on the son's head;
Trapped in suits and litigations,
Of decrees and attachments that village was.

Farms had green wheat,
Zizyphus fruits in bushes;
Of cucumbers and melons,
And of sour tamarinds that village was.

Tinkling bangles,
In veils was the modesty;
Hissing and screeching at the crack of dawn,
Of a few milestones that village was.

Spinning the hand wheels,
Singing sweet lullabies;
With hair grown jute-like
Of such grannies that village was.

Hand ground,
Cooked with love and care;
Of tamarind and chilly sauce,
Of bread browned to crispness that village was.

(6)

धँसी आँखों और सूखी पसलियों का गांव था,
गांव था, वह कोढ़ वाली उँगलियों का गांव था।

लाल बहियों में रहन थे, खेत सारे गांव के,
जाल में घर–घर फंसा था, मकड़ियों का गांव था।

कर्ज़ दादा का पिता पर फिर पिता का पुत्र पर,
वादों, प्रतिवादों मुकद्मों कुर्कियों का गांव था।

खेत में गेहूं हरे थे, झाड़ियों में बेर थे,
ककड़ियों का और खट्टी इमलियों का गांव था।

चूड़ियों में खनखनाहट, घूँघटों में लाज थी,
पो फटे चलती हुई कुछ चक्कियों का गांव था।

कातती चरखे, सुनाती थी जो मीठी लोरियां,
सूत जैसे बाल वाली नानियों का गांव था।

हाथ से पीसी, पकाई जो किसी ने प्यार से,
कैंथ की चटनी, करारी रोटियों का गांव था।

(7)

Tear-streaked cheeks of the Moon,
Must have cried before he slept;
These stars are the tear drops of the Moon,
How sorrowfully he must have wept.

    In the goblet of eyes flourished,
    The blooms of moonlight;
    Did you sow the Moon
    In the ambrosial soil of your heart!

Night sits solitary on the shore,
Leaving tresses of winds at large;
You and the night must have washed,
Your own moons in the dark.

    Unable to hold the wind's finger,
    Wandered away the poor infant;
    In the crowded carnival of clouds,
    The Moon must have gone astray.

You could not have slept,
And the window lay open in the room;
On sleepy, drowsy eyelids,
You must have carried the Moon.

(7)

गालों पर गीली रेखाएँ रोकर सोया होगा चाँद,
ये तारे हैं चाँद के आँसू कितना रोया होगा चाँद।

फूल चाँदनी के महके हैं आँखों के गुलदस्तों में,
मन की चन्दनियाँ मिट्टी में तुमने बोया होगा चाँद।

रात अकेली तट पर बैठी खोले केश हवाओं के,
अपना तुमने और रात ने अपना धोया होगा चाँद।

छूट गई तर्जनी हवा की था अबोध वह बिछुड़ गया,
मेघों के इस भीड़ भरे मेले में खोया होगा चाँद।

खिड़की खुली हुई होगी और नींद नहीं आई होगी,
अलसायी बोझिल पलकों पर तुमने ढोया होगा चाँद।

(8)

Ever since the courtyard's gulmohur
Was torn by the riots
It feels as if someone has decapitated
The head of my Home.

The roof leaks,
Cracked are the walls;
Whenever the rain falls,
I worry about my house.

How deep indeed,
Are these enchanting eyes of yours;
I fondly call them,
The blue ocean of my Home.

That when I returned
After many days of roaming,
Oh! I cannot explain
How ill was the temper of my Home!

Threshold is dolorous,
Gloomy are the closed doors;
Not just of only one
But such is the tale of every home.

The festival wears candles,
Whenever it comes;
Radiance has of late become
The ornament of my home.

(8)

कटा है जबसे फ़सादों में गुलमुहर घर का,
लगा है काट दिया ज्यों किसी ने सर घर का।

छतें टपकती हैं, दीवारें दरकी रहती हैं,
लगा ही रहता है बारिश में मुझको डर घर का।

हैं कितनी गहरी तुम्हारी ये मदभरी आँखें,
पुकारता हूँ इन्हें नीला समन्दर घर का।

कि जब मैं लौटा था परदेश से कई दिन में,
बयान क्या करूँ, उफ! कैसा था तेवर घर का।

उदास देहरी है गुमसुम हैं बन्द दरवाज़े,
ये एक घर का नहीं, किस्सा है ये घर घर क़ा।

दिये पहनता है त्यौहार जब भी आता है,
उजाला बन गया है इन दिनों ज़ेवर घर का।

(9)

There was criticism,
Also the complaints to woo;
Many were the blessings
And good wishes too.

This is how I travelled,
Through the thorny highways;
Elders' hands to drive,
Fuel was their prayers.

This darkness my friends
It could do no harm!
Someone's prayers were with me
Like companions by my side.

Who could have busted,
My body's fragile fort!
Triumphant flags of your memories,
Were with me afloat.

Right here was everything,
But you were not;
With me was the sky
As were the four directions!

(9)

साथ थे शिकवे गिले आलोचनाएँ साथ थीं,
थे कई आशीष भी, शुभकामनाएँ साथ थीं।

इस तरह तय हो सका काँटों भरा यह पथ यहाँ,
हाथ सर पर था बुजुर्गों का, दुआएँ साथ थीं।

यह अँधेरा कुछ न कर पाया हमारा दोस्तों,
हमसफ़र बनकर किसी की प्रार्थनाएँ साथ थीं।

किस तरह फिर ध्वस्त होता देह का जर्जर किला,
ज़ब तुम्हारी याद की पीली ध्वजाएँ साथ थीं।

था सभी कुछ तो यहाँ पर एक बस तुम ही न थे,
आसमाँ भी साथ था, चारों दिशाएँ साथ थीं।

(10)

The sight of them no more incites
The waving of handkerchiefs from windows;
The cities are not gratifying,
As they were in the days of yore.

Ice does not melt from the mountains,
No more falls the Moon;
Seeing their smiles now,
No earthquakes boom.

Such things happen,
Whenever changes the time;
There are no sails,
Though boats you do find.

It was mandatory earlier
To sing within their range;
But nobody harmonizes now,
With their cadence.

Celebrations and birthdays,
Do long for friends;
No more on feasts and festivals,
Are presents exchanged.

The spring of colours,
walks stealthily into homes now;
Pigments not besmeared,
no more are played, drums and diphthongs.

The cheeks may laugh aloud,
They can smile full length;
Such is the era now-a-days
That nobody is prosperous and content.

(10)

उन्हें देख कर अब खिड़की से हिलते हैं रूमाल नहीं,
शहरों में अब पहले जैसा होता इस्तकबाल नहीं।

नहीं पिघलता बर्फ पहाड़ों का, गिरता है चाँद नहीं,
अब उनकी मुस्कान देखकर आता है भूचाल नहीं।

जब भी वक़्त बदलता है कुछ ऐसा ही हो जाता है,
नावें तो मिल जाती हैं पर होते उन पर पाल नहीं।

पहले उनके सुर में कई सुरों का मिलना लाजिम था,
आलापों पर उनके अब देता कोई भी ताल नहीं।

इन्तज़ार रहता है, उत्सव, वर्षगाँठ पर यारों का,
त्योहारों पर उपहारों से अब सजते हैं थाल नहीं।

दबे पाँव आ तो जाता है घर में रंगों का मौसम,
बजते नहीं ढोल और ताशे उड़ता कहीं गुलाल नहीं।

चाहे जितना भी हँसलें, मुस्का लें जीभर कर गा लें,
यह है ऐसा वक्त आजकल कोई भी खुशहाल नहीं।

(11)

Wet wood, kitchen, tongs,
Cutter, stove and smoke;
Moisten collyrium, clinking bangles,
This gorgeous doe and smoke.

Memories of mother's home,
Aflame in heart's alcove;
Oozing from eyes,
The soul's sandal and smoke.

The blessings of the elders,
His siblings' nagging strokes;
Sweet is the beloved's home,
Hazy mirror and smoke.

On the henna painted hands,
That's what the destiny wrote;
Grindstone, fodder, broom, sand,
Pots, fuel and smoke.

Saffron, henna and lac,
Toe-rings, anklets, nose-pin in trove;
These are bridal assets,
Pangs, perplexity and smoke.

Fast offered to the goddess,
Fragrance rises from alcove;
Incense, garlands,
Turmeric paste and smoke.

(11)

गीली लकड़ी चूल्हा चौका चिमटा बेलन और धुँआ,
भीगा अंजन, बजते कंगन यह गोरा तन और धुँआ।

यादें पीहर की सुलगी हैं धधक उठी हैं सीने में,
आँखों से बाहर निकला है मनका चन्दन और धुँआ।

सास ससुर की आशीषें हैं ननद देवरों के ताने,
साजन के घर भला लगे है धुँधला दर्पण और धुँआ।

मेंहदी रचे हुए हाथों पर लिखा यही अब किस्मत ने,
चक्की चारा झाड़ू बर्तन मिट्टी ईंधन और धुँआ।

कुंकुम मेंहदी और महावर बिछुए पायल नथ मुँदरी,
दुल्हन की सौगातें हैं ये तड़पन उलझन और धुँआ।

सन्तोषी माता का व्रत है महक उठे हैं आले में,
अगरबत्तियाँ पुष्पहार हल्दी का ऐपन और धुँआ।

(12)

The trees are sad,
In silence lie the leaves;
The dew-drenched garden,
wore the butterflies.

Trapped in smoke,
Is the capital's sky;
Wearing wrinkles,
The morning sun arrives.

Something must have forced,
The cosmetic make-up;
Why else did the river wear,
Wave-kneaded scallops.

People did not have,
Even rags for their bodies;
But when the Lord came marching by,
Cloth-flags were fluttering in the colonies.

Such was the status,
Displayed by mountains in the rains;
On their heads they wore,
Caps starched and strained.

(12)

उदास पेड़ हैं पत्तों ने चुप्पियाँ पहनी,
ओस में भीगे गुलिस्ताँ ने तितलियाँ पहनी।

धुएँ में घिर गया आकाश राजधानी का,
सुबह के सूर्य ने चेहरे पे झुर्रियाँ पहनी।

सिंगार करना विवशता कोई रही होगी,
नदी ने गूंथ के लहरों में सीपियाँ पहनी।

नहीं था चाहे बदन पर लिबास लोगों के,
हुजूर आए तो बस्ती ने झण्डियाँ पहनी।

दिखाया मर्तबा बारिश में इन पहाड़ों ने,
सरों पे अपने कलफ़दार टोपियाँ पहनी।

(13)

This unworthy Fall
Has shaken the shoulders of the Sun;
And the mendicant sunlight
Kept beating the bowl of the Sun.

Perhaps written on it,
Are the songs of the pink dawn;
Pinning high were the hopes,
But blank was the canvas of the Sun.

Sometimes in the camps of the clouds,
Sometimes behind the mountains;
Wistfully gazed the hungry plants,
At this official tour of the Sun.

Swallowed so much of the darkness,
Yet the face was not blackened;
Buzzing around from town to town,
Was the yellow drone of the Sun.

Its clout is confined,
Only to the dark and dainty tresses;
The pounding wind could not deal
Any harm to the Sun.

(13)

पतझड़ की इस अनऋतु ने कन्धा झकझोरा सूरज का,
मँगती सी यह धूप बजाती चली कटोरा सूरज का।

शायद इस पर लिखे हुए हों गीत गुलाबी सुबहों के,
सोचा था लेकिन निकला है कागज़ कोरा सूरज का।

कभी बादलों के शिविरों में, कभी पहाड़ों के पीछे,
देख रहे भूखे पौधे सरकारी दौरा सूरज का।

इतना पिया अँधेरा फिर भी चेहरा नहीं हुआ काला,
भिन्नाता है नगर नगर पर पीला भौंरा सूरज का।

है केवल पहचान इसे काले घुँघराले केशों की,
कुछ भी नहीं बिगाड़ सका है पवन झकोरा सूरज का।

(14)

He will rise up,
With tight fists and stout stand;
Someone will stand up again,
Holding the mighty pen.

He who got estranged once,
On an unknown curve;
Will come forth one day,
And stand firm.

Finding fruit laden trees,
Any stranger or passer-by,
Will stand up
Stone in hand.

Though you buried your conscience,
In the broad daylight;
It will rise and come,
Out of the grave at night.

The sunflower which, like a proud knight,
From dawn to dusk, did blossom,
Shall bow his head down
When the sun is veiled behind the twilight.

(14)

मुठ्ठियों को बाँधकर तन कर खड़ा हो जाएगा,
फिर यहाँ कोई कलम लेकर खड़ा हो जाएगा।

जो न जाने कब अजाने मोड़ पर बिछुड़ा कभी,
एक दिन वो सामने आकर खड़ा हो जाएगा।

देखकर फलदार शाखों को कोई भी अजनबी,
लेके अपने हाथ में पत्थर खड़ा हो जाएगा।

रोशनी में चाहे दफ़ना तो दिया तुमने ज़मीर,
रात को वह कब्र के बाहर खड़ा हो जाएगा।

था सुबह से शाम तक जाँबाज़ जो सूरजमुखी,
जब ढलेगा दिन झुका कर सर खड़ा हो जाएगा।

(15)

Come O' traveller
Let us go.
Far is the home
Let us go.

Earned a lot of Silver,
Were lost hither-thither;
Now some prizes we must forgo,
To find Self – Let us go.

The sun hides his face,
Bent are the flowers low;
Ill omens are getting this place,
Hurry up – Let us go.

The fruit laden trees,
Are assaulted again;
Here you are ineligible O' tyro.
Rush, Flee – Let us go.

Those visible around,
Are faces fake and trite;
Ours may rather stay indoors,
Save your face, O' traveller,
Let us go.

(15)

चलो मुसाफिर, लौट चलें,
दूर बहुत घर, लौट चलें।

पाकर, भटके यहाँ वहाँ
अब कुछ खोकर, लौट चलें।

आफ़ताब ढल गया, झुके,
फूलों के सर, लौट चलें।

फिर फलदार दरख़्तों पर,
उछले पत्थर, लौट चलें।

बाहर झूठे चेहरे हैं,
अपने अन्दर, लौट चलें।

(16)

Foreordained were
The calamities for me;
Etched was the alienation
On the face of my destiny.
    Downright untenable,
    On the very face;
    Such were the verdicts
    Slapped on my fate.
What time could manage
To write for me
Were caravans of pains and plights -
That was my portion
    The ones which were
    Marked by the poacher;
    Such were the nests,
    That came to my share.
Long were the episodes,
Planted in my Life's charter,
Of this uncouth
And arrogant weather.
    Pertaining to these plebeians,
    Who were fear-bound;
    Were the only issues,
    Accrued on my account.
There were many there,
Who were clear favourites;
But only the jealous,
Fell to my lot.
    On every step
    Though there were debacles,
    I was blessed by Providence
    With courage and guts.

(16)

ज़लज़ले मेरे मुकद्दर में लिखे,
फ़ासले मेरे मुकद्दर में लिखे।

जो किसी भी हाल में वाजिब न थे,
फ़ैसले मेरे मुकद्दर में लिखे।

वक़्त ने दुश्वारियों के दर्द के,
काफ़िले मेरे मुकद्दर में लिखे।

कहकशां की थी नज़र जिन पर यहाँ,
घोंसले मेरे मुकद्दर में लिखे।

बेअदब गुस्ताख़ मौसम के कई,
सिलसिले मेरे मुकद्दर में लिखे।

उस रियाया के, जो थी दहशतज़दा,
मसअले मेरे मुकद्दर में लिखे।

थे कई ऐसे जो ख़ासमख़ास थे,
दिलजले मेरे मुकद्दर में लिखे।

हर कदम पर चाहे थी नाकामियाँ,
हौसले मेरे मुकद्दर में लिखे।

(17)

I would live with a smile,
If you give ever one sad afternoon,
I will drink, if you fill,
A glass of afternoon.

When the eclipse nibbles the sun on solstice,
The day shall advance;
The afternoon shall observe fast,
She will worship the sacred basil plants

Swear it O' Sun,
You won't chase the clouds and wander;
Don't you depart the forlorn afternoon,
Lest she will renounce and go asunder.

In this weather imbued with,
The sick and fatigued violet clouds;
Like the pale lips of green Neem,
The thirsty afternoon spouts.

The crow squawked on the parapet,
Perhaps arrives the epistle from amour;
On toes sits the impassioned afternoon,
Awaiting someone on the door.

(17)

जी लेंगे हम भी दे देना हँसकर एक उदास दुपहरी,
पी लेंगे हम भी दे देना भर कर एक गिलास दुपहरी।

सूरज को जब ग्रहण लगेगा दिन बैसाखी पर सरकेगा,
तुलसी की पूजा कर लेगी रख लेगी उपवास दुपहरी।

बादल के पीछे मत जाओ, सूरज तुम्हें शपथ है इसकी,
तुम बिछुड़ोगे तो वियोग में ले लेगी सन्यास दुपहरी।

थके थके बीमार बैंगनी मेघों वाले इस मौसम में,
हरे नीम के होंठों की पीली पपड़ायी प्यास दुपहरी।

कौआ बोला है मुँडेर पर शायद प्रेमपत्र आएगा,
दरवाज़े पर इन्तज़ार में बैठी है बिन्दास दुपहरी।

(18)

When time could not change,
The rules of storms;
How then could it alter,
These lamps' customs and norms.

> Whereupon were distanced many friends,
> Did come such turns along;
> I carried through the rules
> Of separation, all my life long.

The poor nest did not know,
One day it will burn to ashes;
So horrifying would be,
The dictates of lightning flashes.

> Breaking all bounds he moved forward,
> When pestered by hunger and privation;
> Remained buried in the books,
> All the virtual's rules and regulations.

Removed the curtains, sometimes,
Concealed the tears in shadows;
With age have been changing,
The customs and canons of the windows.

> What a weird city is this!
> Everywhere there is smoke and haze;
> Moods and tempers like jungles,
> Lunatic wolves' rules and rage.

(18)

वक़्त के साथ बदले नहीं आँधियों के नियम कायदे,
फिर बदलते भला किस तरह इन दियों के नियम कायदे।

मोड़ ऐसे भी आए कई हमसफ़र दूर होते गए,
हम निभाते रहे उम्र भर दूरियों के नियम कायदे।

आशियाँ को नहीं था पता एक दिन राख हो जाएगा,
इस तरह होंगे दहशत भरे बिजलियों के नियम कायदे।

तोड़कर सब हदें बढ़ गया भूख ने सब सताया उसे,
कागज़ों में लिखे रह गए रोटियों के नियम कायदे।

चिलमनों को हटाया कभी आँसुओं को छिपाया कभी,
उम्र के साथ बदला किए खिड़कियों के नियम कायदे।

किस तरह का शहर है यहाँ हर तरफ है धुँआ ही धुँआ,
जंगलों की सी आबो–हवा भेड़ियों के नियम कायदे।

(19)

What is eating the sun,
Its halo appears emaciated!
Helpless is the light,
By darkness is it intimidated!

Letters of which are faded,
Pages that are torn;
Light is but a chapter,
Of that book of dawn.

This is an eclipsed day,
Pale is its tired face;
Light is but the community
Of scattered rays.

Sky swarmed by kites,
Earth is besieged by vultures;
Does light stand for
The funeral pyres burning yonder?

This is an astounding tale,
From the sun's court;
The light has been hitherto swallowing,
The injustice in its own fort!

You may agree or not, that is your right,
But, in my opinion,
Giggling and chortling children,
Are the true synonyms of light.

(19)

सूरज को हुआ है क्या कृशकाय उजाला है,
डरता है अँधेरे से, असहाय उजाला है।

अक्षर हों मिटे जिसके पन्ने हों फटे जिसके,
उस धूप की पुस्तक का अध्याय उजाला है।

ये ग्रहण लगा दिन है पीला सा थका चेहरा,
जर्जर हुई किरणों का समुदाय उजाला है।

चीलों से भरा नभ है गिद्धों से घिरी धरती,
क्या जलती चिताओं का अभिप्राय उजाला है।

यह बात है अचरज की सूरज की कचहरी में,
जो सहता रहा अब तक अन्याय उजाला है।

मानो या न मानो तुम मेरा तो यही मत है,
हँसते हुए बच्चों का पर्याय उजाला है।

(20)

Just observe the heels and fingers,
Look at his eyeballs and frown;
Come let us survey the ribs
Of this dilapidated town.

What! Has the blood been frozen?
Why doesn't it seethe and roar?
Come let us see the veins and arteries
Of these blind streets and roads.

When there is nothing worth seeing,
Why stay, come let us go.
They used to gleefully giggle once,
Just note those sullen windows.

Oh! Where are they?
The black haunting eyes, the dusky faces?
Time has grown old
Just observe the wrinkles.

Quite possibly there still remain
A few more chopped heads;
Come let us carefully scan,
The colonies which are long dead.

(20)

एड़ियों को पुतलियों को, उँगलियों को देख लें,
आओ इस जर्जर शहर की पसलियों को देख लें।

खून को क्या हो गया है। क्यों नहीं आता उबाल,
बन्द गलियों की नसों को, धमनियों को देख लें।

देखने को जब यहाँ कुछ भी नहीं है तो चलो,
खिलखिलाती थीं कभी उन खिड़कियों को देख लें।

अब कहाँ वो सुर्मई आँखें वो चेहरे सन्दली,
वक़्त बूढ़ा हो चला है, झुर्रियों को देख लें।

बहुत मुमकिन है बचे हों कुछ कटे सर और भी,
आओ हम अच्छी तरह से बस्तियों को देख लें।

(21)

I am embalmed in your fragrance,
With me are your remembrances;
Who says I am alone in my odyssey,
Your eyes navigate my passage.

I am not an aspirant of light,
Nor am I host to the moonlight;
I am at peace even in the dark,
With me are the galactic lights.

Storms cannot bend me,
Can lightning leave me aggrieved!
I am a sapling tendered by blessings,
Your prayers are with me indeed.

Though estranged I am not lost,
O' Life I haven't forgotten your plights;
I am a tiny, twinkling lamp,
With me are dark nights.

In Time's eternal links I repose trust,
Abiding is my faith in the innocence of moments;
I am a bird that is soaring,
With me are these winds.

(21)

मैं घिरा हूँ तेरी खुशबुओं से, तेरी यादें मेरे साथ हैं,
मैं अकेला कहाँ हूँ सफ़र में, तेरी आँखें मेरे साथ हैं।

मैं नहीं मुंतज़िर रोशनी का, मेज़बाँ मैं नहीं चाँदनी का,
हूँ अँधेरे में भी मुतमइन मैं, कहकशाएँ मेरे साथ हैं।

आँधियाँ क्या झुकाएँगी मुझको, बिजलियाँ क्या डराएँगी मुझको,
मैं दुआओं का सींचा शजर हूँ, प्रार्थनाएँ मेरे साथ हैं।

मैं बिछुड़ कर भी बिछुड़ा कहाँ हूँ, ज़िन्दगी तुझको भूला कहाँ हूँ
टिमटिमाता हुआ इक दिया मैं, स्याह रातें मेरे साथ हैं।

है यक़ीं वक़्त की शख़्सियत पर, ज़र्द लमहों की मायूमियत पर,
इक परिन्दा हूँ उड़ता हुआ मैं, ये हवाएँ मेरे साथ हैं।

(22)

The linseed through its blue eyes,
Glanced at the flowers of mustard;
In the green field, without binging,
The mustard blooms swayed like drunkards.

Tied in nuptial knot
The wind sailed over the track;
Yellow faced mustard flowers,
Flickered in steps.

These are the moneylenders,
In the habit of recovering interest;
These mustard flowers chase the spring,
Like a merchant in pecuniary quest.

Who knows they may catch,
A damsel's overture;
These swindler mustard flowers,
Greedily await such junctures.

They heard abuses of the weather,
And took insults in their stride;
How wonderfully lived the mustard flowers,
Enlivening the fields' Socratic pride!

(22)

नीली आँखों से अलसी ने देख लिये सरसों के फूल,
हरे खेत में बहक उठे हैं बिना पिये सरसों के फूल।

हवा बँधी परिणय बन्धन में गुज़र गई पगडण्डी से,
पीले पीले चेहरे वाले हिला किये सरसों के फूल।

ऋणदाता हैं ब्याज वसूली करने की आदत इनको,
पीछा करते हैं बसन्त का ये बनिये सरसों के फूल।

शायद किसी किशोरी की वेणी आमन्त्रित इन्हें करे,
इन्तज़ार करते रहते हैं ये छलिये सरसों के फूल।

मौसम के अपशब्द सुने अपमान सहा हँसते हँसते,
खेतों के सुकरात बने क्या खूब जिये सरसों के फूल।

(23)

Wish I could find
At least one lamp aglow;
That I may espy
One familiar face in town.

Strange faces made of stone,
Sitting atop the wooden torsos;
Would that I might see
At least one living soul!

What is wrong with the garden
Tears of dew are flowing free;
Wish I could see at least one flower,
Dispersing the seeds of glee!

Darkness, your memories,
And silence looms;
I might just see the road,
If you rise and shine O' Moon!

Amongst these changing
Faces of clouds;
At least one face akin to you,
Wish I could find out.

(23)

कोई चराग़ तो जलता दिखाई दे जाए,
शहर में कोई तो अपना दिखाई दे जाए।

काठ के काँधों पे पत्थर के अजनबी चेहरे,
आदमी कोई तो ज़िन्दा दिखाई दे जाए।

क्या हुआ बाग को बहते हैं ओस के आँसू,
कोई एक फूल तो हँसता दिखाई दे जाए।

तीरग़ी है, तेरी यादें हैं और सन्नाटा,
चाँद तू आए तो रस्ता दिखाई दे जाए।

बादलों के ये जो बनते बिगड़ते चेहरे हैं,
काश चेहरा कोई तुझसा दिखाई दे जाए।

(24)

Sits tight-lipped,
Meets extremely cautiously;
The Time, now-a-days,
Meets in changing guise.

> It is too busy
> To meet useless people;
> But goes an extra mile,
> To those who can serve a cream truffle.

This moon in its lunar prime,
Is the prized silver coin;
And when ever it is pleased,
Meets me with welcoming warmth.

> Face of this governance,
> Does stay in the sunshine,
> But a strange darkness is found
> Behind the closed doors of the Palace.

On the surface, the river water
May look like a mirror,
But under the lotus blossoms
Looms the mud's ugly face.

(24)

रहता है चुप्पियाँ साधे बेहद सँभल के मिलता है,
यह वक़्त आजकल हमसे चेहरे बदल के मिलता है।

उसको फ़िजूल लोगों से फुरसत नहीं है मिलने की,
पर जिनसे उसका मतलब है बाहर निकल के मिलता है।

ये है जो चाँद पूनम का चाँदी का एक सिक्का है,
होता है जब मेहरबाँ ये, हमसे उछल के मिलता है।

चेहरा तो इस हुकूमत का रहता है धूप में लेकिन,
इक अजनबी सा अंधियारा पीछे महल के मिलता है।

चाहे हो आईने जैसा दरिया का ऊपरी पानी,
कीचड़ का गन्दला चेहरा नीचे कमल के मिलता है।

(25)

Calamities befell one after another,
The road was paved with corpses;
Black ominous birds swarmed,
The town's sky on all axes.

I don't know what flashed in the memory,
When shadows were getting shy;
Green hyacinths webbed all over,
The water of limpid eyes.

The day Yudhistir's picture
Was removed from his room,
He turned into a messiah
And was surrounded by the headlines.

Till there was a single breath in balance,
Everybody stood on the bank;
But once reduced to a corpse
He was surrounded by boats on all flanks.

That which bore fruits,
Had to suffer the stones;
And the tree that bestowed cool shelter,
Was ransacked by saw-hammers and tongs.

He finds the crossroads today,
Such like a *causar* artifice;
Almost like a pawn,
He is cordoned off by the vaulting dice.

(25)

हादसे होते रहे पथ अर्थियों से घिर गया,
शहर का आकाश काले पक्षियों से घिर गया।

जाने क्या क्या याद आया धूप जब ढलने लगी,
आँख का पानी हरी जलकुम्भियों से घिर गया।

चित्र जिस दिन से युधिष्ठिर का हटाया कक्ष से,
वह मसीहा बन गया वह सुर्खियों से घिर गया।

श्वास जब तक शेष थी तब सब किनारे पर रहे,
आदमी वह लाश बनकर किश्तियों से घिर गया।

जिसमें फल थे पत्थरों की मार वह सहता रहा,
पेड़ छायादार था जो आरियों से घिर गया।

आज चौराहा उसे चौपड़नुमा लगता रहा
गोट बनकर वह उछलती कौड़ियों से घिर गया।

(26)

Those who jovially
Embraced you with a song;
Were actually heart broken,
And woebegone.

Kindness on them
Could never shine,
Yet everybody called them
Sublime!

Only those who opted
On wrong paths to drive;
In this demoniacal era,
Do prosper and thrive.

Those who have dark areas
In their life everywhere;
Started preaching us,
And became our advisors.

Where can one go?
This City has become a jungle;
Hither serpents,
Thither Mongooses dwell.

(26)

जो खुश होकर लगे तेरे गले हैं,
असल में ग़मज़दा हैं, दिलजले हैं।

भलाई से न जिनका वास्ता है,
उन्हें सब कह रहे कितने भले हैं।

ग़लत थे रास्ते जिनके यहाँ पर,
वो ही इस दौर में फूले–फले हैं।

भरे है ऐब जिनकी ज़िन्दगी में,
हमें उपदेश वो देने चले हैं।

कहाँ जाएँ, शहर जंगल बना है,
कहीं विषधर कहीं पर नेवले हैं।

(27)

Where the childhood was spent,
I have turned away from that pavilion;
I am deeply scared that
I have lost my home in oblivion.

I am not deserving
Of these swinging urban taverns,
My lips have forgotten
Their smiles endearing.

Of the branch that was cut,
I am the bird who's lost lien;
Forgotten have I now,
My relations with that old banyan.

Being turned to stone now
No more do I fear tragedies,
Forgetting how to shed tears
In this course of adversities.

I may well come and listen
To your sermons too,
Though my hands have quite forgotten
How to clap or to boo.

(27)

जहाँ बचपन गुज़ारा वह ठिकाना भूल आए हैं,
बहुत दहशतज़दा हैं आशियाना भूल आए हैं।

शहर की इन थिरकती महफिलों के हम नहीं क़ाबिल,
हमारे होंठ अपना मुस्कराना भूल आए हैं।

कटी जो शाख़, हम उस शाख़ से बिछुड़े परिन्दे हैं,
अब उस बरगद से हम रिश्ता पुराना भूल आए हैं।

हुए पत्थर, नहीं अब हादसों की फिक्र है हमको,
ग़मों के दौर में आँसू बहाना भूल आए हैं।

सभा में, आपकी तक़रीर सुनने आ तो जाएँगे,
मगर ये हाथ अब ताली बजाना भूल आए हैं।

(28)

There is another cast
Behind your facade;
When could the mirror of your room,
See that face apart.

Everybody in your coterie,
Was surprised at your silence;
Nobody could construe truly,
The language of your eyes.

Do your fellow passengers,
Know and have this presage;
On the very next turn
The road will part ways!

You are a fair-weather river,
Flowing and bathing the braes;
The clairvoyant has deciphered,
The script your palm displays.

The ocean shall welcome you
with wide open arms;
why then is your heart
Gripped in ominous qualms!

(28)

तेरे चेहरे के पीछे है जो तेरा दूसरा चेहरा,
उसे कब देख पाया है तेरे कमरे का आईना।

तुझे चुप देखकर हैरान थे सब तेरी महफ़िल में,
समझ पाया नहीं कोई तेरी आँखों ने जो बोला।

तेरे हमराह जो हैं, क्या उन्हें मालूम है इतना,
जो अगला मोड़ आएगा अलग हो जाएगा रस्ता।

किनारों को भिगोती एक बरसाती नदी है तू,
नजूमी ने बताया पढ़ के तेरे हाथ की रेखा।

करेगा बाँह फैलाए समन्दर तेरी अगवानी,
नदी तू क्यों ठिठकती है तेरे मन में है डर कैसा।

(29)

I must admit
It was strangers who heaped praise;
But from our very own
I received only hate.

God knows how dismal
His poor fate was!
In the pouring rain he got
A cracked roof on top.

Friends made him
Feel threatened here;
Shelter he found,
In the enemies' lair.

Only after my voice
Had grown hoarse here,
Did they find time
To lend me an ear.

Him the banks accorded
A hearty welcome
And the Boat was duly tendered
Garlands of honour and pride.

(29)

यह माना परायों से शोहरत मिली थी,
मगर ख़ास अपनों से नफ़रत मिली थी।

न जाने उसे कैसी किस्मत मिली थी,
जो बारिश में टूटी हुई छत मिली थी।

था ख़तरा उसे दोस्तों से यहाँ पर,
जो दुश्मन थे उनसे हिफाज़त मिली थी।

गला रूँध गया था यहाँ जब हमारा,
उन्हें बात सुनने की फुरसत मिली थी।

किया ख़ैरमक़दम किनारे ने उसका,
शिकारे को भरपूर इज़्ज़त मिली थी।

(30)

It was after ages,
That I could locate his home;
He met me like a stranger,
Who was shadow of my own.

I knew not where to,
That bird had flown;
In the courtyard I found,
A broken feather alone.

Where have I come,
With my head that is brittle;
Everybody bore stone in hand,
With whomsoever I mingled.

The envelope sent to me,
Contained paper that was blank;
I could easily discern the reply,
To the letter I had sent.

Everywhere were scattered,
The sunlight's feathers;
I found him soaked in blood,
The bird of Day was butchered.

(30)

बाद मुद्दत के उसका मुझे घर मिला,
यार मेरा वो अनजान बन कर मिला।

वह परिन्दा तो जानें कहाँ उड़ गया,
मुझको आँगन में टूटा हुआ पर मिला।

सिर मैं शीशे का लेकर कहाँ आ गया,
जो मिला मुझको लेकर के पत्थर मिला।

कोरा कागज़ लिफाफे में भेजा मुझे,
पढ़ लिया मैंने ख़त का जो उत्तर मिला।

धूप के पंख बिखरे थे चारों तरफ,
दिन का पक्षी मुझे खून में तर मिला।

(31)

How strange this evening is,
Colourful smoke flies;
As if a carnival of kites,
Is being held in the sky.

Try and unfold
The sleeves some day;
You will find the den,
Where the venomous serpents stay.

Safe is this throne of theirs,
They fear no danger;
They know the cryptic gates,
Leading to the caves of treasure.

This musical soiree of theirs,
Is bereft of any rhythm;
There is only cacophony here,
Of rough and cracked drums.

These burning homes and blood stains,
Are mere political fun-game;
Fools are you who think,
Riot is their name.

They stay close,
But keep their hearts distant;
This is the concise preface,
Of those who are our confidants.

(31)

न जाने शाम ये कैसी धुँआ उठता है रंगो का,
लगा हो जैसे इस आकाश में मेला पतंगों का।

कभी तुम खोल करके देख लेना आस्तीनों को,
तुम्हें मिल जाएगा डेरा वहाँ काले भुजंगों का।

कोई ख़तरा नहीं महफ़ूज़ है उनका ये सिहांसन,
उन्हें मालूम है रस्ता ख़ज़ाने की सुरंगों का।

बिना सुरताल की है उनकी ये संगीत की महफ़िल,
यहाँ तो बेसुरा सा शोर है फूटे मृदंगों का।

ये बिखरा ख़ून, जलते घर, मनोरंजन सियासत का,
हैं मूरख आप जो देते इसे हैं, नाम दंगो का।

रहें नज़दीक लेकिन मन में अपने दूरियाँ रक्खें,
यही संक्षिप्त परिचय है हमारे अन्तरंगों का।

(32)

This is a journey of
A few untold stories;
This life is nothing but,
An odyssey of melancholies.

Her eyes
Sailed in the blue sky;
The boats sailing through
The deserted Nile.

Attires of smoke,
Fire to drape;
The colony had seen,
Journey of torches aflame.

She was with me,
And darkness around;
How wonderful was,
The stairwell's round.

Wish that childhood,
Could come back;
That we may again undertake,
The journey of laps!

(32)

है अनकही कुछ कहानियों का सफ़र,
ये ज़िन्दगी है उदासियों का सफ़र।

उनकी आँखें, ये आसमाँ नीला,
सूने दरिया में किश्तियों का सफ़र।

पैरहन थे धुएँ के, आतिश के,
देखा बस्ती ने तीलियों का सफ़र।

साथ उनका था और अँधेरा था,
कितना अच्छा था सीढ़ियों का सफ़र।

काश फिर लौट आए वो बचपन,
तय करें फिर से गोदियों का सफ़र।

(33)

This life has been spent,
In the lonely ghettos;
I had to live here,
With the mere shadows.

Time kept descending,
Into the blind vales;
In the depths were deposited,
Memories' echoing wails.

I came across many days,
That played notes of mourning;
With the clarinet were spent,
A few moments that will stay.

The sky is sitting sullen,
With its back turned on Him,
Ever since the moon awoke,
Stretching its limbs.

Swinging trees,
Streaming curls and pins;
Don't know when they vanished away,
With the vagrant winds.

(33)

यह ज़िन्दगी अपनी कटी तनहाइयों के साथ,
रहना हमें पड़ा यहाँ परछाइयों के साथ।

ये वक़्त घाटियों में उतरता चला गया,
यादों की गूँज रह गई गहराइयों के साथ।

मातम की धुन बजाते हुए दिन कई मिले,
कुछ लमहे बिताए यहाँ शहनाइयों के साथ।

पीठ उसकी ओर मोड़ के बैठा है आसमां,
जबसे उठी है चाँदनी अंगड़ाइयों के साथ।

हिलते हुए दरख़्त बिखरते हुए गेसू,
ओझल न जाने कब हुए पुरवाइयों के साथ।

(34)

It is evening again
The darkness intensifies;
Heart glooms for no reason,
The soul grows listless.

You are not the only one here,
Who is perplexed;
On every home's roof,
Sadness has made its nest.

The face I had kept somewhere,
And long forgotten about,
Met me after ages,
To look and stare.

Whose hearts are vitriolic,
And minds full of notoriety;
Flowing from their lips,
Pompous stream of love and piety!

He may be standing,
On a towering hill,
But in the hands of the storm,
The tree is a mere puppet.

(34)

फिर शाम हो गई ये अँधेरा घना हुआ,
मन बेवजह उदास हुआ अनमना हुआ।

तू ही नहीं है एक मुसीबतज़दा यहाँ,
हर घर की छत पे दुख का बसेरा बना हुआ।

चेहरा जिसे मैं रख के कहीं भूल गया था,
मुद्दत के बाद उससे मेरा सामना हुआ।

जिनके दिलों में मैल है ज़ेहन में खुराफ़ात,
उनके लबों पे प्यार का झरना बहा हुआ।

चाहे खड़ा है वो किसी ऊँचे पहाड़ पर,
आँधी के हाथ में ये शजर झुनझुना हुआ।

(35)

He may have been uncouth, Sir,
Raw and undeveloped,
But, in this city he was
The cynosure of a hundred eyes.

He did not bow his head,
To the courts and clouts;
He was not a sunflower,
But a firm palm spout.

This span could not recognize,
How brilliant he was!
Diamond of first water,
But hidden under the dust.

Nobody accorded him here
The honour he deserved;
From this world's gimcrack vanity,
He was distant and reserved.

The moment veil of darkness was lifted,
Morning donned nuptial attire;
Red was the spangle on forehead,
Pink vermilion setting hair on fire.

(35)

चाहे हुज़ूर आदमी वह बेशऊर था,
इस शहर की वह सैकड़ों आँखों का नूर था।

उसने झुकाया सर नहीं दरबार में जाकर,
सूरजमुखी का फूल नहीं, वह खजूर था।

यह वक़्त उस ज़हीन को पहचान ना सका,
वह ग़र्द में छिपा हुआ इक कोहिनूर था।

उसको यहाँ किसी ने भी इज़्ज़त नहीं बख़्शी,
वो दुनिया के इन ढोंग दिखावों से दूर था।

हटते ही तीरग़ी के सुहागिन हुई सुबह,
बिंदिया थी लाल और गुलाबी सिंदूर था।

(36)

For those with deep roots,
Storms evoke no fear nor strain;
Those with enduring colours,
Have nothing to shy from the rain.

The one who always casts
His eyes on the backs of friends,
And one who ambushes others,
Has no fear of treacherous attack.

To welcome whom even
Darkness bows its head;
Those dyed in soot of disgrace,
Dark night cannot make afraid.

Those who understand all the moves,
Of the pawn and horses alike;
Why should they fear the defeat of checkmate,
For whom life is just a game of chess.

It was the others,
Who burnt down the nests;
Why should they fear revenge,
Who only stood and stared.

(36)

जड़ें जिनकी हों गहरी उनको झंझावात का क्या डर,
है जिनके रंग पक्के उनको इस बरसात का क्या डर।

नज़र रहती है अक्सर दोस्तों की पीठ पर जिसकी,
जो करता वार छिपकर उसको भीतरघात का क्या डर।

अँधेरा जिनकी आगवानी में सर अपना झुकाता है,
जो खुद कालिख में लिपटे उनको काली रात का क्या डर।

जो पैदल और घोड़ों की सभी चालें समझते हैं,
है जिनकी ज़िन्दगी शतरंज उनको मात का क्या डर।

वो कोई और थे जो बस्तियों को राख कर आए,
तमाशा देखते थे जो उन्हें प्रतिघात का क्या डर।

(37)

The person whose existence now,
Is a sight intolerable for many;
Their own henchmen, once he did,
Collaborate in their felony.

> Why do you beg before an assassin,
> Expecting mercy from a slayer?
> What worth are these tears,
> In this callous abattoir.

Those whom he supported
Whenever they stumbled;
They only laid stones,
On the path he travelled.

> Empty shall remain the hands,
> When both for heavens depart;
> Be it pauper or an emperor,
> Can you tell them apart!

Hold him in awe,
Badger not the innocent;
One moan of his unleashes,
A hundred curses incessant.

(37)

जिस शख़्स का वजूद है उनकी निग़ाह में,
शामिल रहा था वो कभी उनके गुनाह में।

क्यों माँगता है रहम की तू क़ातिलों से भीख,
इन आँसुओं का मोल कहाँ क़त्लगाह में।

कठिनाईयों में उसने सहारा दिया जिन्हें,
पत्थर बिछा रहे थे वो ही उसकी राह में।

दोनों जहाँ से जाएँगे खाली रहेंगे हाथ,
क्या फ़र्क़ राहगीर में और शहनशाह में।

उनसे डरो, सताओ नहीं जो निरीह हैं,
हैं बद्दुआएं सैकड़ों उनकी कराह में।

(38)

Somewhat frightened,
Is the twilight this dawn;
Seems as if the darkness,
Has made some mistake.

The day of eclipse,
Helpless is the sun,
The golden glow has been,
By the darkness, made to run.

These homes sit,
With heads bent down;
Mournful shadows,
Lie scattered over the town.

Like a tassel of wool,
The light is entrapped;
As a broken withered cord,
In shreds the wind is snapped.

Weird is the game of colours,
Played by the spears and lances;
Blood on the walls and floors,
The colony was painted red.

(38)

सुबह की धूप कुछ सहमी हुई है,
अँधेरे को ग़लतफ़हमी हुई है।

ग्रहण का दिन, बहुत बेबस है सूरज,
सुनहरी रोशनी काली हुई है।

ये घर बैठे हैं अपने सर झुकाए,
शहर में मुर्दनी छाई हुई है।

उजाला ऊन सा उलझा हुआ है,
हवा ये डोर सी टूटी हुई है।

निराला फाग खेला बर्छियों ने,
लहू से लाल ये बस्ती हुई है।

(39)

He came with stones,
In disguise of flowers;
He mouthed such words,
Which injured the core with power.

Who had been lost,
Estranged in mob of clouds;
He came with ocean in eyes,
That moon in yellow shrouds.

On whom till yesterday,
Shut were the palace's doorway;
He has been escorted in,
By the transformed time today.

The window opened,
Poured in the envelop of sunshine;
This sun has descended today,
With destiny that brightly shines.

When you finally came O' Rain,
This languid forest then,
Brought in your welcome,
Crowns of the trees, slain.

(39)

जो लगते फूल जैसे ऐसे पत्थर ले के आया है,
जो करते घाव गहरे ऐसे अक्षर ले के आया है।

बिछुड़ कर बादलों की भीड़ में गुम हो गया था जो,
वो पीला चाँद आँखों में समन्दर ले के आया है।

जिसे कल तक मिले थे राजपथ के बन्द दरवाज़े
ये बदला वक़्त उसको आज अन्दर ले के आया है।

खुली खिड़की, लिफ़ाफ़ा धूप का आकर गिरा भीतर,
ये सूरज आज तो उजला मुक़द्दर ले के आया है।

तू जब आ ही गई बरसात तो मजरूब ये जंगल,
तेरे स्वागत में पेड़ों के कटे सर ले के आया है।

(40)

Began with denial,
Became consent;
Burns like cinder now,
Now a shower of rain.

It was a wilted tree,
Bearing fruits in animation!
Worshiped by all now,
Becomes a godly incarnation.

He was exalted enough,
Amongst the midgets;
Becomes a character now,
Very special, of the puppets.

Annoyed with the sun was,
The darkness's sovereignty;
Truth in the bastion of lies,
Became a sinful entity.

Now you open your windows,
With care and caution;
Razor-edged this moon,
Has these days become a weapon.

(40)

इन्कार से शुरू हुआ, इकरार बन गया,
अंगार बन गया, कभी बौछार बन गया।

सूखा हुआ दरख़्त था फलदार बन गया,
सब उसको पूजने लगे अवतार बन गया।

बोनों के बीच उसकी बहुत पूछ हो गई,
कठपुतलियों का ख़ास वो किरदार बन गया।

सूरज से थी नाराज़ अँधेरे की हुकूमत,
सच झूठ की बस्ती में गुनहगार बन गया।

अब तुम सँभल के खोलना अपनी ये खिड़कियाँ,
तीखा ये चाँद इन दिनों हथियार बन गया।

(41)

They carried on making
Glass houses;
Kept on hiding,
Heads made of wax.

These messianic sailors,
With the boats of clay;
Kept on ferrying the meek,
Across the river bay.

Kept on debating,
The sun in vain;
There were trees alone,
To clap and acclaim.

The panting daylight,
Ran helter-skelter;
Celebrating the fest,
Were the ravenous vultures.

Observing the city
Drenched in blood,
Red flowers of Gulmohur
Had reason to laugh.

(41)

काँच के घर बनाते रहे,
मोम के सर छिपाते रहे।

नाव मिट्टी की ले नाख़ुदा,
पार दरिया कराते रहे।

सूर्य तक़रीर करता रहा,
पेड़ ताली बजाते रहे।

हाँफती दौड़ती धूप में,
गिद्ध उत्सव मनाते रहे।

गुलबदन शहर को देखकर,
गुलमुहर मुस्क़राते रहे।

(42)

The roads are with us
So are the stumbling blocks,
Adversities attend on us
Also awaits us our destination.

Whilst living with friends,
This lesson was well-learned;
If hopes are with you,
Tragedies also happen.

Saturated remain their eyes,
With smoke of darkness;
Desires do sleep beside
The tosses and turns of duress.

In the binding folds of life,
Lie the pages of days and nights;
Radiance of celebration booms,
Also on heel is the pitiable plight.

Echoing in the vales,
The voice ricocheted back;
Alive are the passions,
And distances yet uncovered.

His sights are set on the sky,
And on his lips are prayers;
The efforts are untiring,
And there's courage enough to dare.

(42)

रास्ते भी साथ हैं और ठोकरें भी साथ हैं,
मुश्किलें भी साथ हैं और मंज़िलें भी साथ हैं।

दोस्तों के साथ रहकर यह सबक उसको मिला,
आसरे भी साथ हैं और हादसे भी साथ हैं।

उसकी आँखों में भरा रहता अँधेरे का धुआँ,
ख्वाहिशें भी साथ हैं और करवटें भी साथ हैं।

ज़िन्दगी की ज़िल्द में हैं रात और दिन के सफ़े,
रौनकें भी साथ हैं और गर्दिशें भी साथ हैं।

घाटियों में गूँजकर आवाज़ वापस आ गई,
चाहतें भी हैं और फ़ासले भी साथ हैं।

उसकी नज़रें आसमां पर उसके होठों पर दुआ,
कोशिशें भी साथ हैं और हौंसले भी साथ हैं।

(43)

In the city again,
Hissing are the gales freak;
Cut are the fingers,
Again on this street.

Even flowers have become,
So razor sharp,
That butterflies are feeding,
On wounds and gall!

They have ushered in,
A new dawn;
All around are burning,
The old inhabitations.

They never could see,
The virtues indeed;
Always finding,
The faults and defeats.

Cordoned by axes and saws,
This tree is under house arrest;
Search and explore O' bird,
A new abode for your nest.

(43)

फिर शहर में चली आँधियाँ,
फिर गली की कटी उँगलियाँ।

फूल भी इतने तीखे हुए,
ज़ख़्म खाने लगी तितलियाँ।

लाए हैं वो उजाला नया,
हर तरफ़ जल रही बस्तियाँ।

खूबियाँ उनको दीखी नहीं,
ढूँढते वो रहे ख़ामियाँ।

यह शजर आरियों से घिरा,
खोज पंछी नया आशियाँ।

(44)

She had no feud with me,
There was no disdain;
The sky was clear,
There was no sign of rain.

I had already
Bent down so low,
There was no further scope
To stoop any more.

I had lived in darkness
Throughout my life;
And held no wish,
Or desire for the light.

With broad smiles did I,
Bid her adieu;
No binding interest had she,
That could entice her in lieu.

Abundant in heart were,
Emotions and pains;
Ash was aplenty,
But there were no flames.

Someone assiduous there was,
But only yonder;
No effort on this side,
Nobody to ponder.

It was only me,
Crooning on the stage;
Though there were no demands
Of the time and age.

(44)

उनको मुझसे कोई रंजिश नहीं थी,
आसमां साफ था बारिश नहीं थी।

मैं पहले से ही इतना झुक चुका था,
और ज़्यादा तो गुंजाइश नहीं थी।

उम्र भर मैं अँधेरे में रहा था,
रोशनी की मुझे ख़्वाहिश नहीं थी।

मुस्कुरा कर उन्हें रूख़सत किया था,
लौटने की कोई बन्दिश नहीं थी।

दिल में जज़बात तो बहुत से थे,
राख ही राख थी आतिश नहीं थी।

था उधर ही कोई करमफरमां,
इस तरफ़ से कोई कोशिश नहीं थी।

वो मैं ही था जो ग़ज़लें गा रहा था,
वक़्त की कोई फरमाइश नहीं थी।

(45)

I suddenly woke up,
Shaken out of existence;
Ever since I looked
Into the mirror of my conscience.

    How could he be convicted,
    For his sins and errors!
    He inhabited after all,
    The capital of the emperor.

The trees have been culled,
And transformed into chairs;
What ties have they now,
With the birds flying high.

    He was standing sullen there,
    A ghost pondering alone;
    He was living history,
    Of some tragic bygone.

Why do you wait for him,
Who has been left behind?
As I staggered on my journey,
The highway questioned me.

(45)

मैं जागा नींद से हिलने लगा वजूद मेरा,
कि जब से आईना मैंने ज़मीर का देखा।

गुनाह करके सज़ायाब किस तरह होता,
जहाँपनाह के आला शहर का बाशिन्दा।

दरख़्त कट गए तब्दील कुर्सियों में हुए,
अब उनका उड़ते हुए पंछियों से क्या रिश्ता।

खड़ा हुआ था वहाँ चुप सा उल्टे पैर लिये,
था वो इतिहास किसी दर्दनाक माजी का।

क्यों इन्तज़ार है उसका जो पीछे छूट गया,
सफ़र में रास्ता मुझसे सवाल कर बैठा।

(46)

Left abaf were eaves and corridors,
Homes and farms;
Also left behind,
Were trails of wet soles.

Soared so high,
The birds of eyes;
Left in the rear,
Were all seven blue skies.

When became apparent,
The truth that was bitter;
Vanished was the generosity,
Of the impostors and mimers.

I walked past them,
Smiling in disdain;
All the arrogant rouges,
Were dumped away in drain.

Who were hitherto emperors,
Have today become paupers;
Snatched are the castles and palaces,
Estranged are the well-wishers.

(46)

छज्जे, गलियारे, मकान पीछे छूटे,
भीगे पाँवों के निशान पीछे छूटे।

इतने ऊँचे उड़े परिन्दे आँखों के,
सातों नीले आसमान पीछे छूटे।

तल्ख़ हक़ीक़त जब हो गई नुमायाँ तो,
बहूरूपिये मेहरबान पीछे छूटे।

हम हँस कर उनके आगे से निकल गए,
सभी बेअदब, बदजुबान पीछे छूटे।

कल जो बादशाह थे आज फ़कीर हुए।
क़िले, महल और निगहबान पीछे छूटे।

(47)

There were glowing candles,
Chandeliers shone;
Shrouded in darkness though,
Were the crowns and thrones.

Frail and impoverished,
Rag-worn were the masses;
Adorned with silk and gems,
Were the emperors' dresses.

Ashen faces,
Gripped in a scare,
Covered in veils,
Deep in despair.

For the love of country,
Who got their heads slain;
No one to commiserate with them
in their grief and pain.

Proclaiming shamelessly now,
Are the emperor's commanders-
"The martyrs of the war
Were jinxed and sinister."

(47)

रोशनी थी, शमाएँ थीं, फ़ानूस थे,
तीरग़ी में मगर तख़्तेताऊस थे।

थी रियाया फटेहाल और अधमरी,
रेशमी, हुक्मरानों के मलबूस थे।

ख़ौफ़ खाए हुए सन्दली चेहरे,
चुनरियों से ढके कितने मायूस थे।

सर वतन के लिए जो कलम हो गए,
दर्द उनके, किए किसने महसूस थे।

शाह के सिपहसालार कहते हैं अब,
जंग में काम आए वो मनहूस थे।

(48)

How could he win,
In this weird era;
Who was made of elixir,
And did not have poison-aura.

Though there wasn't any,
Dilemma or difficulty;
Tough was the journey,
Living for him was not easy.

Smiles were
Artificial braces;
Masked were
All the faces.

Crucial decisions of home,
Were refrained;
Down and out were the elders,
Lonely was their domain.

Despondent in its own home,
Remained the orphan light;
On the father sky it had,
No claim, no right.

How could he be bestowed,
With honour and applause;
He was neither a charming lily,
Nor and ornamental rose!

(48)

इस युग में वो सफल नहीं था,
जो अमृत था, गरल नहीं था।

चाहे कोई ख़लल नहीं था,
फिर भी जीना सरल नहीं था।

मुस्कानों में नकलीपन था,
कोई चेहरा असल नहीं था।

घर के अहम फैसलों में,
बूढ़ों का कोई दख़ल नहीं था।

आफताब का आसमान में,
अपना कोई महल नहीं था।

उसको इज़्ज़त कैसे मिलती,
जो गुलाब या कमल नहीं था।

(49)

The darkness came on roll,
With the Sire's arrival in town;
The serpents stirred their hoods,
Snake charmers paced up and down.

Altered is the river's face,
Awe-struck are the fish;
The brae can now see,
The greedy fishermen feverish.

The colony is victim of bestiality,
Terrorized are the streets;
Roaming unabashed are,
The swindlers and bandits.

They have no permanent homes,
Now here and now there;
Life in their camps moves,
Only when they migrate, the gypsies.

Someday the foul weather will surely change,
And this long dark night will end;
Giving way to a new dawn,
Which we fondly hope to see.

(49)

हुज़ूर आए, हुई शहर में शुरु अँधेरों की चहलक़दमी,
हिलाए साँपों ने फन हवा में, बढ़ी सपेरों की चहलक़दमी।

हुई है दहशतज़दा मछलियाँ, बदल गया है नदी का चेहरा,
किनारे अब देखने लगे हैं, यहाँ मछेरों की चहलक़दमी।

दरिन्दगी की शिकार बस्ती, हैं ख़ौफ़ खाये हुए मुहल्ले,
यहाँ खुलेआम हो रही है ठगों–लुटेरों की चहलक़दमी।

नहीं है इनका कोई ठिकाना, कभी यहाँ हैं, कभी वहाँ हैं,
हमेशा ख़ानाबदोश रह कर हुई है डेरों की चहलक़दमी।

कभी तो बदलेगा बिगड़ा मौसम, ढलेगी ये लम्बी रात काली,
है हमको उम्मीद, देख लेंगे, नये सवेरों की चहलक़दमी।

(50)

Sheared from torsos,
Will be the proud necks;
Shoulders will no more,
Bear the arrogant heads.

They remained always,
Bowed in your service;
The fragile necks never did
Stand arrogantly upright.

May you O' Lord,
Live forever—
Thus was the clamour
Of eulogy on every tongue.

Whenever he desired,
Howsoever the Sire wanted;
Turned all necks in tandem,
Meekly bowed and slanted.

When the King's cavalcade,
Marched past the street;
Peeped from the windows,
The neck heavy with greed.

(50)

धड़ से हटाई जाएँगी शहज़ोर गर्दनें,
काँधों पे रह न पाएँगी मुँहज़ोर गर्दनें।

ख़िदमत में आपकी ये हमेशा झुकी रहीं,
तन कर कभी नहीं रहीं कमज़ोर गर्दने।

आलमपनाह! उम्र आपकी दराज़ हो,
हर ओर कर रही हैं यही शोर गर्दनें।

जब जब भी, जिस तरह से भी, चाहा हुजूर ने,
आदाब करके मुड़ गई उस ओर गर्दनें।

निकला जुलूस कूचे से जब ताज़दार का,
खिड़की से झाँकने लगीं बिल्लौर गर्दनें।